LIFE: a variant of adventure

an anthology of short stories
by Sandra Joy

First published in September 2022 by
Kani Consultants, Newcastle, Australia.

Edited by S. Boyd
First printed by Lightning Source

ISBN: 978-0-6450773-0-8

NATIONAL
LIBRARY
OF AUSTRALIA

A catalogue record for this
work is available from the
National Library of Australia

Dear reader

I hope you both laugh and cry because that's

LIFE: *a variant of adventure.*

Contents

Shoes   1
Who's the foreigner?   9
Bloody school   15
Death kills   19
The sleepover   31
That night   41
Farewell cases   45
Belt up   53
Drunk as a hoot   59
Don't let them see   63
Here we go again   73
Driving lessons   81
Supping above the canopy   85
The case against short platforms   91
Tosser child   95
Reasons to live   99
Evidence   103
Waking for adventure   107
Country love stars   111

Shoes

Another contract. Another party. Another band to see. Dinner with the family on Thursday and I must pick up those navy-blue Baby-Doll shoes before the show on Friday night. Life as a London model is chaotic.

Promotions for Fashion Week are on every magazine cover and store window, and thoughts outrun my feet on the way to my agent's office.

'Hi Pam.' Receptionist Charlotte longs to walk the runway herself. She copies fashion trends and hangs out with the 'right' people, just hoping to be discovered one day. 'Samantha is a little late, she's held up in a meeting. Oh, did you see that psychic we talked about?'

'I sure did, but I don't think my reading is as believable as yours. Apparently, I will *"Travel abroad and marry someone whose name starts with the letter E"*.' I mock. 'No chance!'

We are interrupted by my self-assured agent. I'm sure her spine has been fused straight, just to highlight the pulled tight hair. Her whole persona is for one purpose – to reveal her solemn face so that everyone sees what expression she has for them. Always the boss.

'Pam, I am so sorry for being late, the designer made some changes to the run sheet and so we needed to change your contract.'

'What?' The familiar frustration rising. 'Not again. How can he keep doing …'

'Pam, settle. He wants *you* to be the lead model on the catwalk for the Harrods' Annual Parade. *The* most prestigious event of the year. Pam, this really puts you on the map!'

Without moving to her office, she places the contract on the reception counter and mocking calmness adds, 'Only if you want it.'

Even Charlotte looks genuinely excited for me as she hands me a pen.

My entire body quivering, I try to scribe my name. 'Well, I hope they never question this, 'cos that does *not* look like my signature.'

Both types of ecstasy keep me high for the full twenty-two minutes' drive. I can't wait to tell Mum and Dad about this. My brother Pete will laugh, but later he'll tell me he's proud.

The mood is noticeable as soon as I open the front door. It's quiet and sombre, not the usual happy chaos. And somehow the house looks bare, but I can't quite work out why.

I find Mum in the kitchen and our expression and insight meet before our arms do. 'Mum, what's going on?'

'Sit down, sweetheart.'

Expecting me for dinner, Dad is already seated, and both were too distracted for the normal courtesies. Within minutes they proceed to tell me about an idea they have been discussing for a while. It's a wonderful job opportunity to work on an exciting major construction project.

'We're moving to Australia so Dad can work on the Snowy Hydro Project.'

'But that's the other side of the world!' I doubt they need a geography lesson from their nineteen-year-old daughter, but how else does one react to news like that?

'Pam,' Mum started, squirming for a reason that was soon to be revealed, and waiting to gauge my reaction to the news before asking me the next question. 'Pam, can we please buy you a ticket.'

The tears don't match my anger; the confusion doesn't match my words.

How am I to choose between a career and my family? How can parents expect that of me? I cannot believe this would be put on me.

Turning absentmindedly, my body has decided that my mind wants to leave, and I head to my car.

I can't tell anyone at first – hoping to wake from this nightmare. I avoid my family for a few days until I realise that I already miss them and so I should enjoy what time we have before they go. The reminder of them leaving hurts too much so I then withdraw again.

I party too hard and drink too much and try to resume work as normal, but that doesn't feel right either.

Then on the first of December, as the London Christmas lights turn on, I know I couldn't spend these significant occasions without my family. I am moving to Australia.

The FareSea docks in Sydney five months and eleven days after that fateful conversation, four weeks and six days after leaving my home. I know, I marked every day on my wall calendar, counting down to the end of my life. The end of my career, my friends, my place on the modelling and social ladders.

Over the next few months, I watch Dad adjust to his new career, laugh at Mum struggling with the "Australian version of the English language" and listen to my brother talk about the "hot chicks".

Mum and I have taken to window-shopping after the stores close. This way we can take it all in without looking like tourists, allowing us to appear more "local" when we encounter other residents.

'Pam look at this,' Mum points to one of the many signs taped on a glass window, 'A fashion parade. Not quite the same standard as you're used to, but why not give it a go. It would give you something to do and who knows, it might open up a few doors. You may even get some work out of it.'

I baulk at the idea, but the flier is now glued on the walls of my mind. The only way I had been able to accept moving to Australia was to completely leave my past behind, consciously closing all doors with the hope of one day finding and opening new ones.

'Mum …'

'Just think about it.' And we move to the next window.

Those words are typical of the magic that mothers have. *'Just think about it.'* And now I cannot *stop* thinking about it.

A week later, Mum and I go into David Jones to buy school shoes for my brother. Whether or not Mum chose the time and venue deliberately I will never know.

'That's $3.85 thank you,' the sales clerk told announced. 'I am sure your son will find them comfortable. Now, at the risk of being intrusive, may I please ask whether this young lady would consider being in our fashion parade next week. We are still taking entrants and she definitely has the height and figure to show our clothes well.'

Before either of us could say anything, she turns to me and added, 'Don't worry, Miss. Our co-ordinator Mary will take you through the process of walking a runway. Catwalks are not that scary once you've done it a few times and you can practice before the event.'

It's the paradox that makes me change my mind. I have never experienced nerves in a show, having been told on many occasions that I am 'a natural' on the runway. So the idea of being allowed to practice to stop me being scared makes me laugh inside. I imagine it being like visiting kindergarten as an adult.

'Why not. I would love to.'

She calls for Mary, who invites me to come back tomorrow morning for a fitting and then to go around the corner to be sized for matching shoes.

'The owner of Mason's Shoe Store helps us every year. He knows the styles and colours for this event, so will show you your options.'

Mary hands me three slips of paper, each detailing the clothes I will be wearing. I am to give them to Mr Mason, who will fit me with three pairs of shoes to match. After the fitting, it is his responsibility to deliver them all to the hall on the morning of the show.

I couldn't be so lucky. Surely the attractive young man behind the counter can't be the one required to tend to my needs.

'Good afternoon.' I mutter, 'I'm here to see the owner, Mr Mason.'

'I'm his son, how can I help?'

I hand him the papers and he hands me a pair of knee length stockings then politely directs me to a seat.

'He won't be long.'

Crossing my knees to place the second stocking on, a sturdy pair of legs arrives in front. Peering upwards as I sit back, I am pleasantly surprised to see the young salesman again. Deftly he was balancing a pair of navy-blue Baby-Doll shoes across the back of his forearm like a waiter with a wine bottle, displaying them for me to see. Were they glossy or were his eyes glistening and reflecting in them?

'May I help you with these? I'm your assistant today, my name is Errol.'

Down on one knee, he places the shoes on the floor and takes my right calf in his left hand. Nervously yet skilfully, he places my foot into my favourite style of shoe. The butterflies in my stomach echo the words of the psychic, 'You will travel abroad and marry someone whose name starts with the letter E'.

'M'am,' he was saying as I regain composure, 'Would you like to try the other one and walk around in them? And m'am,' his eyes pierce through mine to my heart, 'Would you please go out with me?'

We marry five months later. On this beautiful Australian day I wear those same navy-blue Baby-Doll shoes, but tonight he takes them *off* my feet.

Who's the foreigner?

This story was first published in 2021 in an anthology Memory in Lockdown: Creative Nonfiction.

Isn't it funny how we believe the things we are told without questioning them? This photo has been on a wall in every one of our family homes — and there's a lot of them, but that's another story. The verbal caption has always been that it's my mother, 'On the ship, coming out to Australia from England when she was twenty'.

Now, I know it's my mother. She was, after all, my mother for nearly fifty years. But that doesn't prove that everything I know about this photo – or her – is true.

Let's start with the fact that she's not actually *on* the boat. She's sitting on a railing on the dock. Maybe they took their luggage on board and came off again for a final photo. I don't know the sequence of events, but this photo is not taken "on the ship" as I was led to believe.

I was eleven when I first noticed this photo. Mum was more than willing to reminisce about her homeland and the trip abroad. It was her twentieth birthday and, back then, it was customary for birthdays to be celebrated at the captain's table. So Mum, her older brother, and their parents were invited to dine in the prominent area of the dining hall – along with a bunch of strangers also born on that day.

As a teenage girl, this story took my imagination into fantasy land. For a long time, I dreamt of dining with the captain of a grand ship – though in my mind, we were all celebrating my twenty-first birthday and the young captain fell in love with me. There's something way more romantic about my version of the story. But then, reality isn't always perfect.

Apart from the lie that was told, I like this photo of Mum. She's very pretty, and very happy. I have no doubt that the smile on her face would have been directed at a male. You see, my grandmother was the world's biggest flirt. She used to brag about having three dates on the same night. At least Mum pretended to be a prude my entire life. She always went to church, she would ignore me for days if I liked the wrong guy; and clothes, jokes, and manners were all very old-fashioned. And I know why − shame! That's right. Shame.

When I was in my early thirties, I came across some details that caused me to question the innocence of my mother.

Fact: My mother had her twentieth birthday on that ship, 21 January 1950.

Fact: My parents were married on 14 October 1950.

Fact: My oldest sister was born on 16 May 1951.

My mother moved to the other side of the world and, within nine months, travelled, met a man, fell in love, and got married. Back in 1950, that was okay, not uncommon. My sister was born, full-term, seven months later! Back in 1951, that was *not* okay, that was *not* common.

Three thoughts punished my mind. How did my strict Catholic mother get pregnant before she was married? How did I live in this family for thirty-two years and not know? And, what other secrets did my family keep stowed away from *the baby*?

I wonder what other adventures of immorality she experienced. Being so beautiful, it wouldn't be hard for her to attract men. Before coming to Australia, she was a London model. Apparently, she modelled for some high-class store; Harrods or something. I can't recall.

Mum raised her first two daughters to be truly fashionable young ladies. I have seen slides and photos of them when they were little girls, parading around in their lacy dresses and white frilly socks. When they weren't riding horses or wearing school uniforms, they wore the same style – and always had bags, gloves, and shoes to match.

I think the novelty wore off, or Mum finally accepted that London was a long way away, because, by the time she got to me, Mum no longer imparted her fashion skills. It must have been hard to recreate the London look when your makeup is rolling off from perspiration, or the flies are sticking to it. Living on the land, they only went to town once a month and, depending on the land, money grew short. Mum struggled, but never complained. She was strong. Instead, she turned her skills to making her home beautiful, and became very creative with the few resources she had.

So, the only deportment training I got was, 'You can wear lipstick when you're thirteen'. That was it. No training in fashion, style, or grooming. No array of clothes or accessories for me. So, I grew up not caring. It was all just to make you look good for other people anyway, and I was happiest in the countryside on my own.

When it came to learning about fashion, I missed the boat, but genetics speak loudly. Mum had a very narrow waist – typical of her time, and a feature of models back then. She passed that on to me, though I tend to hide it with the flabby results of junk food. My daughters both have it too, and they are stunners. Mum didn't teach them about makeup either, instead she just lectured, 'You're too young to wear that!' Thankfully, they grew up with friends who taught them all the girly stuff like clothes, makeup, hair, and accessories. It's funny that they both look like their nanna, yet they both look so different.

Now, my walls have only a few photos of my children and grandchildren and they are all beautiful in their own way. No-one has photos of me, I don't allow it. Photos hold memories of things that aren't true. These images are distorted or interpreted incorrectly. I don't like photos.

Unlike my mum, I have never travelled outside of this country. Yet, somehow, sometimes, I feel like I am the real foreigner.

Bloody school

This story was inspired by the survival heartache of the American school shootings like the 'Florida Massacre'. While many children died, my heart cries for the children who witnessed the event.

'Cassie, I yelled at Oscar.' Sniff. 'And now he's gonna be sad all weekend.'

Cassie is my bestest friend, so she knows how much I love my little brother. Even though she doesn't love hers much.

'Oh Emma, my mum will let you talk to him on the phone after school! That will cheer him up.'

I feel sad and today sucks.

'Okay class, because it's raining, we're not going to do our ball games. Instead, you're going to the library with Mrs Austin. Put away your art works and line up at the door. Quietly.'

I write my name at the top of my picture. I have to, or I might not get it back. And this one's for Oscar.

I am the last one to the line, but Cassie is saving a place for me. She holds my hand as we walk through the school.

Library is always fun. Mrs Austin reads *Possum Magic*. Then we get to pick our own book and read alone. Cassie picks *Blinky Bill* and I pick *The Cat in the Hat*. We are both good readers.

We plop ourselves together on the red beanbag under the biggest window.

"It is fun to have fun but you have to …"

BANG!

I drop the book when I hear Mrs Austin scream.

BANG. BANG. BANG. BANG. BANG.

I scream too, but nothing comes out.

A man is jumping from side to side and there's bright lights coming from that thing in his hand. My friends are falling over. This isn't good. I'm scared.

'Mummy!' I yell but my mouth won't work, and my legs won't work and …

I'm stuck in this beanbag staring at that bad man. I can't move.

I want my mummy.

He's not a man. That's Adam. That's Cassie's brother, Adam. 'No Adam. Stop. Too loud.' I know he can't hear me.

I wish my mouth worked.

'Cassie,' I kinda cough it out. It doesn't sound like me, but it is. 'Cassie,' I turn around to my best friend and quietly scream again.

She looks like my rag doll, but she's all red and sticky. I'm sticky. I try to wipe the sticky stuff off her face.

What's wrong with Cassie?

I don't like this. I cuddle her and close my eyes and try to go to sleep. When I wake up, this won't be real anymore. Cassie is asleep. I wish I was asleep too.

'Hey there.' The big lady sounds nice like Mum. And she has a badge. 'You're okay now. How about you come with me.'

I nod a little bit then shake Cassie to wake her up. She can't stay alone, she'll be scared.

The nice lady takes both my hands and says the other lady will get Cassie.

She picks me up just like mum does.

She hugs like mum.

'I want my mummy.'

'I know darling. Let's go find her.'

'But she's not at home. And Cassie's asleep. And Adam is naughty. And Oscar is still sad cos I haven't given him his picture yet. And I want my mummy. Cassie has to wake up soon cos I'm sleeping at her place and I have to talk to Oscar after school.'

Death kills

This story was first published in Memory in Lockdown: Creative Nonfiction, in 2021

The first death I experienced was my own. That's a true story. The next death I experienced was my daddy's ... and I killed him. That's almost a true story.

Although my mum was a London model, my dad was a farmer to the core. Hard work and long hours were all he knew, and I don't think I ever saw him in anything but moleskins, R.M. Williams boots, and his Akubra hat.

Dad's father had a sheep farm outside of Singleton. He wanted to raise cattle, but his bank manager friend convinced him that, 'The financial future of Australia is in sheep'. So, Pop invested in sheep – and went broke. Someone told me that he then changed banks and stopped buying the guy beer on Friday nights. Anyway, to get out of debt, Pop opened a shoe store at The Entrance. I have no idea how that transition of product, location and lifestyle came about; I just know it to be a crucial part of my existence.

I didn't get to meet my dad's parents, but I'd heard that my father was an only child and his mum apparently died when he was young. So, not only was he close to his dad, but he was also the sole source of labour. As Dad grew, he worked on the farm (which was now growing lucerne and raising cattle) and he worked in the shoe store, travelling between the two as required. My dad was a hard worker.

It was in this shoe store that my parents met. It's a very romantic story (worthy of Hollywood) but it doesn't belong here. For now, just know that they met and had five children. Of these, the first two daughters married and turned my parents into grandparents. Their third child died at the tragic age of three days. After waiting a few years, they had two more children – my brother, Stuart, and another two years later, me.

Between all of this, Dad was finally able to buy his dream property. I don't know how many he looked at, but he narrowed it down to three and took Mum, Stuart and myself to help him make the final decision. Mum didn't like the one with the ugly house, but Stuart wanted its bike tracks. Dad and I both loved the one with the cottage and rose garden but, in the end, he chose Appletree Flat.

Our new home was a forty-minute drive northwest of Singleton, and the two hundred and fifty hectares of prime land was tucked into the base of the mountains of Wollemi National Park. The property had everything Dad ever wanted: paddocks for lucerne and other crops, paddocks for cows and horses, sheds for machinery and hay bales, yards and pens for the chooks and pigs. It even had its own fuel tank, as well as two dams and a creek with a little bridge over it. I saw my first shooting star from that bridge.

My sisters had been into pony clubs and other horse activities, but times were different then. I didn't get to go riding often with my dad, but that's okay. I think that's why I treasure the few memories so much. Whenever we found the time to ride for pleasure, we'd take the horses to the top of a hill and just stop.

'So,' he'd start seriously, 'When you get married, we'll build you and your young man a house over under those trees, and you'll own all that area beyond that dam.'

'You *are* referring to the handsome guy who's going to move in just before I turn eighteen. Totally gorgeous, single and hard-working. The one from the perfect family.'

'Yeah, that's him,' he'd wink. 'And don't forget, ya mum will always expect you for Sunday lunch.'

'We'll be there. Kids 'n' all.'

Dad and I would banter for ages before moving on to the next range where we'd stop and map out another part of our future. It always involved me staying on the land and generations planting roots deep down on Appletree Flat.

As a teenager, I thought this place was perfect. I can only imagine how much my dad loved it.

What's more, to buy this land, he sold the two businesses he created and his other property. For the first time in three generations, this man – my dad – was debt free.

His life was good.

Then he got sick.

Over the next eighteen months, there were many days when Mum and Dad weren't there when I got home from school. They attended a lot of appointments, often travelling to Newcastle or Sydney (with or without us). There was a sudden interest in vegetables and herbal medicine.

Stuart and I both had to go on one of the trips to Sydney to see a naturopath. It was an eerie trip: for the first time ever, no-one was fighting. I read my book, Stuart played with something, and Mum wasn't yelling at Dad to slow down. I think they were preparing us for the disgusting medicine we went home with. Eeyoow! How do they get so much vile into such a small bottle!

The next day, Mum called Stuart and I into the kitchen before dinner and told us to sit down. There was no afternoon tea and no homework; the table was bare, so I was worried. Maybe they'd spent too much on Christmas and we had to forego our pocket-money for a while.

Dad was already sitting in his chair. He spent most of his time in that chair. I'm sure if I looked, it would be faded or dented beneath his mustard-coloured dressing-gown.

Mum stood, leaning against the cupboard beside the stove. I could tell she was pretending not to cry. Neither of them looked at each other.

This was bigger than pocket-money.

It was Mum who told us the details of the secret they'd been keeping for nearly two years. I don't remember her speaking, but I remember what she said. My dad had been diagnosed with sclerosis, emphysema, and asbestosis – a terminal combination of diseases that was causing him to suffer and deteriorate daily.

My dad was dying.

My *daddy* was going to die.

I looked across the table, but he didn't want to look at any of us. My breath had stopped and didn't re-emerge until my body overflowed with gasps for air mixed with bursts of tears. I couldn't stop the tears and I couldn't stop him from dying. This can't be true.

This. Can't. Be. True.

Two weeks later, I started year ten, but I hated being away from Dad. Because we lived so far from town, school days were seven am to five pm. They seemed even longer.

In the second week of term we did a revision test. I knew I didn't want to be at school anymore, and Jenny bragging about beating me on that test was the final straw. I quit.

I returned my textbooks to the supply room, emptied my locker, told my friends, and then told the lady at the office. She called the principal, and I spent over an hour convincing Sister Faith that I would not change my mind, but yes, I would consider coming back next year.

At last, she conceded that I had just unenrolled myself from high school and she asked how I would be getting home. I told her I would catch the bus to my sister's place, and she would drive me home in the morning. I also hoped the moral support would help when I told my parents.

'Okay then,' she offered, turning towards the window that revealed the lines of buses and students. 'Which bus?'

I looked over her shoulder and realised that neither of us had been watching the time. 'That one. The one that just left.'

Sister Faith drove me to my sister's house.

To be with Dad, I left school after doing only four weeks of year ten. I then spent my days at home on the farm. My sixteenth birthday was in February and no-one came. Jenny had a new boyfriend and the group had plans.

The textbooks don't warn you that having a dying father makes you a leper. So, I sat in my bedroom listening to the song, *It's My Party* by Lesley Gore. You probably know it: "It's my party and I'll cry if I want to; you would cry too if it happened to you." I played it on repeat and ate chocolate cake by myself.

When I left my room to get more cake, Dad was back in his chair at the kitchen table. He must have just taken his medication because his breathing was still very deep and loud. I knew this embarrassed him, so I decided that I'd had enough cake, and slipped back to my bedroom without him noticing.

Dad and I spent a lot of time together. One day, when he was still able to drive, he wanted to buy some things from Maitland. I was in the back seat with the windows down, watching and listening. He and the salesman were at the back of the car and Dad was stuttering and stammering, trying to ask for the tractor part the farm needed.

The young salesman was so impatient and rude, mocking Dad for his inability to articulate. I wanted to jump out and hit him! I wanted to yell at that idiot and tell him to be nice because that is my daddy and he is dying. But I was polite. Instead, I got out and walked to the back of the station wagon and told him what Dad needed. From that day on, I became Dad's spokesperson.

For some reason, I was the one person who could understand him. I don't know if I was more determined, or just had better interpretation skills, but nobody was going to insult my father like that again.

On the second of June 1983, we were driving home from Singleton: Mum and Dad in the front, Stuart and I in the back. I don't even know what my brother and I were debating, but I remember Mum turning around and telling me to shut up. Not Stuart. Just me. And it hurt. Worse still, later I was proven to be right (in whatever the dispute was about).

For me, at that time, it was another last straw. Once again, Stuart was the favoured child and, *once again*, I was disregarded.

As soon as we got home, he headed down to the caravan to be with his future wife, Heather. I headed to my bedroom and listened to *Solid Rock* by Goanna.

Then, for some overwhelming reason, I went to my dad's medicine cupboard in the kitchen and took his packet of Serapax. I knew that Dad needed these, but I didn't think of that at the time. *I'm so sorry, Dad.* I went back to the solitude of my bedroom with one thought in my mind – would anyone care if I died?

It wasn't that I wanted to kill myself, I just wanted to know how they would react when they thought I was dead. Would they miss me?

Looking back now, I obviously wasn't thinking clearly or maturely. After all, Dad not having his pills could have killed him and, if taking his pills killed me, I wouldn't be able to see anyone's reaction anyway. But that didn't stop me. I swallowed thirty-one of them.

Heather came into my room unannounced, as she often did. Stuart probably sent her to check on me; sometimes he was nice. She sat on the bed and looked at me, then saw the bottle in my hand. She jumped up and demanded, 'What have you done?'

By this stage I was quite calm (probably sedated) and so I told her: 'I've just taken thirty-one.' Then the thought of getting into trouble entered my mind and I quickly added, 'But please don't tell anyone.'

So ... she didn't.

She went back to the caravan. Back to Stuart.

A short time later, a horrible taste with a hot foam made its way up my throat and I called out to Mum. She panicked and asked the same question.

'I've taken thirty-one of these and I think the coating has come off 'cos it tastes horrible.'

I don't know what she did next, but my brother soon laid me in the back seat of his car and raced me to Singleton Hospital. Apparently, he was pulled over for speeding, but when he explained, the police gave him a lights-and-sirens escort to the hospital. I wish I had seen that, but by the time we arrived, I was clinically dead. They were able to revive me (obviously) and I spent the next seven days in a coma.

I'd never heard of a catheter so, when I finally woke up, I wondered why I didn't have to wee. I laid awake for some time before getting the nurse's attention, watching the monitors and wondering if I was wetting myself. Maybe I had broken that part of me and so I didn't need to wee anymore.

Mum and Stuart visited, so did my sisters and their families, but Dad was too sick to travel. Did he run out of tablets because of *me*? Was he stressed out worrying about *me*? Were Mum and Dad blaming themselves, or each other, for what *I* did?

Dad was now too sick to travel and that's my fault.

So, when the doctor told me that I couldn't go straight home, that they had decided to send me to a psychiatric facility, I was determined to change their mind and get home to my daddy. Before the psychiatrist appeared for his final assessment, I had worked out what he wanted to hear: 'No, I'll never do it again.'

After two weeks in hospital, and a few days of saying the right thing, they gave me permission to go home. Mum had to go to the office to sign the paperwork and collect my belongings. She came back into the ward and explained that they had needed to cut off my clothes to gain immediate access to my chest, so they were disposed of. I fought back the tears over my favourite Johnny Cougar t-shirt, but I was in no position to complain. I couldn't remember what else I had been wearing.

Mum then held up a plastic bag with my twenty-four silver bracelets, leather and silver necklaces and eight silver rings. 'And the lady at the office said to me,' Mum grinned, 'Would you please buy your daughter a jewellery box so she can leave some of it at home.'

I still laugh whenever I put on jewellery.

Because of his breathing difficulties, Dad spent his nights propped up on the kitchen table, trying to sleep. Until that night.

Exactly one month after my overdose, Dad went to bed for the first time in months. In the early hours of the morning, Mum tried to roll him over because he was hogging her side. He wouldn't move. He couldn't move. My dad was dead.

I overdosed on the second of June 1983 and on the second of July 1983 my daddy died. That coincidence haunted me for years. Would he have lived longer if I didn't overdose? I was in a coma for a week, in hospital for a fortnight, but I blamed myself for years that the stress of my actions shortened my dad's life. How much longer would he have been with us if I hadn't been so selfish?

I regressed. My mind wandered back to the period when Dad travelled a lot for his business. I subconsciously told myself that he was away fitting out someone's kitchen, or at a rodeo or getting supplies for the shop. I struggled to accept that my daddy wasn't coming home. Ever. Maybe this was my age, or maybe it was the only way I could cope with the guilt that he'd still be alive if I hadn't been so stupid and selfish. Sometimes I still think that, but mostly now I know it's not true.

At his funeral, my crying became uncontrollable when they lowered his coffin into the ground. With my new thinking that he was only *away*, I couldn't comprehend the funeral and my conscious mind fought back, 'They can't do that to my daddy!'

But they did, and my brother-in-law carried my failing body to the car. Which car? No idea. A car. The car. I didn't care. I wanted my daddy. *I'm so sorry Daddy. I'm so sorry for causing you to die.*

The sleepover

I haven't had a sleepover for twenty years. Well, not with a female. Girls just can't be trusted. They feel entitled. They steal your men.

But Sahra seems trustworthy, even nice. We've worked many nights together, but Tuesdays are slow, so we don't bother going. She isn't like the others. Her sweet demeanour makes her seem genuine and she said she wants to just hang out. Like friends. I'm not even sure what that means, but it would be nice to have a friend so I'm keen to find out. And a little nervous.

A line will help with that. I take the clip bag out of the inner pocket of my handbag. You're kidding; is that all I have left? It's a good thing I'm getting more today.

I tip the remaining half point onto the table and chop it with a credit card. Then I roll up a five dollar note and snort my nerves away.

There are things to do so my home is comfortable for my guest. Clean sheets and an extra blanket on the spare bed. Stock the entertainment – she said she wanted a movie night, so I bought a few more DVDs. We're ordering pizza for dinner, so that's easy.

I remember her saying she likes M&Ms but I wasn't sure what flavour, so I bought three different types. And, of course, plenty of bourbon, coke, and cocktail ingredients. I've ordered the other coke and am picking it up on the way. I know she'll bring a bag of pot. Sahra's *always* got a bag of pot. Before picking her up I spend an hour washing and sanitising the car.

Entering the Caltex, I glance around and park away from the bowsers. Tuesday nights are just the right level of quiet. Not too busy to be seen. Not so quiet as to stand out. A good spot. The Mazda pulls up beside me and both drivers get out for a quick friendly chat. I know this guy – intimately.

The rear passenger window rolls down and a nod invites me to lean in. Cautiously, I dip my finger and have a lick of the product. A tasty lip-numbing justifies me swapping it for $1200. I take my eight-ball of coke, and slide it into my pocket under the guise of removing my car keys.

Before dusk, I wait for Sahra at Wyee Station. I had suggested the 5:20 train, not too early in case we didn't end up having fun and not too late so that wouldn't appear obvious to her.

She arrives with her oversized bright green handbag.

Interesting … no overnight bag for an overnight sleepover? And what is she carrying? If I wasn't parked in a No Stopping zone I could go to help her, but I can't risk turning the car off, so I just help by opening the front door.

She leans in with a 'Hi' and throws all her clothes over the back, covering the floor and seat. Then pours herself into the front seat.

'I've got plenty of Coles bags,' I mock. 'I'll give you a couple when we get home.'

'Thanks! I left in a hurry. I just got away from this guy. What a wank. But he ga' me some buds, so I'm sweet. My feet are killin' me though, bastard wouldn't even drive me to the station!'

While I process this, and move out onto the road, I begin to wonder if she stole all the other things that she doesn't have bags for.

She starts packing her pipe. I am mortified that she doesn't even ask and that she could so willingly risk being caught. My words freeze midway to my mouth.

This is *my* car and I can't even protest. But … she is my guest, and a potential friend, so maybe it's a good thing to be accepting; I can clean the car again tomorrow. Besides, it sounds like she's had a rough day and she obviously can't wait. I wind her window down quarter of the way though, so some of the smoke can blow out.

I just know the stench is penetrating the seat fibres. The mirror becomes useless when she exhales. Worse still, my lungs crave a first drag, not satisfied with a recycled one.

I realise then that, apart from the time spent inhaling, she hasn't stopped talking. 'Plus, I stole these from his girlfriend.' She lifts her leg so I can see the two-inch black heels. 'Any chance you got somethin' comfy I can borrow?'

'Sure. Most o' my shoes are heels or boots, but I think I've got some flats.'

'Thanks mate.' She called me *mate*.

She sucks on her pipe. Her body and brain are so used to marijuana that there is no obvious difference between Sahra stoned and Sahra … I don't think I've ever seen her without those glassy eyes.

'Like me new make-up? K-mart yesterday.'

I steal a quick glance. 'Nice. Love the eyeshadow. Expensive?'

'No idea. I need it. They can afford it.' She hasn't paid for the makeup. This girl is shaping up to be just like the rest of them. Are we really going to be friends? Do I even want to be?

I negotiate my way into the narrow carport and turn the car off. Sahra picks up her handbag, gets out and leans against the car, waiting. No, I am not carrying everything for her.

'I'll give you a hand with your stuff and get you those bags.' So I open the side door and then load my arms. Thankfully, she follows and takes a few things herself.

Inside, I place her things on the lounge, folding a pair of jeans that are aiming for the floor. Sahra tosses her load from the doorway, not caring that it spread all over the lounge and the floor. How on earth did she carry it on the train?

'Beer or bourbon?'

'Ooh, bourbon please!' She looks around. 'Nice place. 'Oh, you've got Californication! Marathon please. I *love* that show.'

'Sounds good. What time do you usually eat?'

'Any time, I'm starvin'. Can I grab a shower first?'

'Of course. It's only a small hot water heater though, so do you mind keeping it short.'

'Yeah, no prob. Thanks.'

We chat for a few minutes about work and her eventful train trip, and decide what pizzas we want for tea. I shouldn't be surprised that she takes her bourbon into the bathroom while I order the pizza. I don't think she has any intention of contributing to the cost. That's okay, I scold myself. She's my guest, so I don't mind. She just seems to take a lot for granted.

I heat the plates in the oven. She's still in the shower. To fill in time I fold her clothes and put them into three green Coles bags, along with the stolen makeup. I place her bags on the kitchen table and bring the plates out to the loungeroom coffee table.

Shortly after, I knock on the bathroom door. 'Pizza's here.'

'Won't be long. Hot water ran out.'

'Wha…! Oh damn. I'm. Sorry.'

I'll be having a cold shower tonight. No apology from her.

Clean and sparkly, she enters my loungeroom just as I insert the first DVD.

'Yum!'

We watch the first two episodes in between pizza, garlic bread, bourbon and bongs. The second episode is on while she bongs and I tidy up. I watch the third and fourth episodes while she texts her friends. *Click click. Tap tap. Bing bing.* She doesn't make a sound, but her phone doesn't stop.

At the end of the sixth episode, I am starting to crash so I change the disc for her and announce I am going to bed. If this is what girls do on sleepovers, I'm glad I usually invite men. Friends are boring.

My body clock wakes me just after seven, hers goes off with the mower next door at nine. I spend two hours trying to keep quiet to let my guest (my new friend) sleep.

I make my bed and remember to find a pair of flat sandals for her.

I straighten the cushions she left strewn across the lounge and floor, then put last night's washing up away and prepare things for breakfast.

When she finally stumbles out, she takes some things from the Coles bags, but it's my handbag behind them that really catches her eye.

'Ooh I like that! Prada! You go girl.'

'Yeah, it's just big enough to keep all the essentials. And it goes with everything.'

'Remind me why you're slummin' it in the 'burbs. You're weird.'

'Gee, thanks.'

We laugh and take our coffees and pancakes outside. For a while we chat about the weather and the lack of plans for the day, and then she announces that she should probably get going.

I rinse the mugs, leave the uneaten pancakes for scraping when I get back, and close the windows. Then I grab my wallet and keys.

'I'll just go to the loo – long trip and I hate train toilets.'

'That's cool. I'll warm up the car.'

I hope it doesn't rain today. I really need to air this car out. Stale pot mixed with human oxygen is *not* a good mix.

As we approach the station she asks, 'Hey, can you stop at the servo? I need a sausage roll an' a can o' coke.'

By now, it doesn't matter that the service station is a kilometre beyond the train station. I am her friend. I am just the chauffeur.

As long as she thinks she has time, I am at her service.

'Sure.'

By the time we get to the train station she has three minutes to get from the car to the platform, but she's not at all concerned. No need to be in a hurry to go … nowhere. I watch her walk up the fifteen steps, across the walkway bridge and down the other side onto platform one, waiting to make sure she's okay.

Just as I hear the train whistle, she looks at me, places her bags on the ground and points at me. It seems odd to be unloading your bags as the train is approaching, so I keep watch. She wants my attention. Is everything alright?

She reaches into a Coles bag and removes a jacket and then lifts out another bag. A black handbag. *MY* black handbag! She waves so sweetly as the train breaks my view of her, that I now doubt what I saw.

I reach for my phone to call her but realise I didn't bring it. Surely she didn't. My hands shake and I start to sweat. Calm down. Get home and confirm this first.

Twelve minutes takes so long.

I was right. The kitchen table is covered with her clothes and my handbag is gone.

'That *bitch*!'

She took my handbag … and everything in it!!! My meds. My diary. My cash bag. Oh, at least that has less than it did this morn … *My coke!*

I can't exactly call the cops. *Oh excuse me officer, a hooker that I invited into my home stole my cocaine.* I'd be the one to end up in jail. Besides, she now knows where I live.

AND she has my shoes.

My whole body tenses and I swipe the plates of pancakes. They head towards the place where my handbag should be and land all over her clothes. And my clean wall.

Shaking, I pick up my phone. 'Hey Mick, it's me. You know that favour you owe me? Well, I have a girl in mind.'

That night

There are two hundred and eleven flowers on the wallpaper opposite my bed. I know, I have counted them many times since that night. *That night*. It seems so long ago, but every time I close my eyes it happens all over again.

Mum taps gently on the door just moments before opening it. She knows I am not getting out of bed to open it. She carries the "sick in bed" tray as my sister calls it and I can smell the pumpkin soup before I even see the steam. With a shy smile she briefly lowers the tray to show me what's on offer before placing it on the desk beside my bed. Beside the soup is a plate with bread cut into thin strips she calls 'soldiers', a bowl with apple pie and custard, and a glass of orange juice.

Dear Mum. Even without knowing the full story, she doesn't seem to tire of this ritual. Mums have instinct. And patience. I am pretty sure she has persisted in bringing me three meals every day since, despite me telling her I don't want to eat. Come to think of it, I am pretty sure I have only eaten two sandwiches and one banana since he left five days and – I glance at the clock – four hours ago.

Oh well. Maybe I will try the soup.

Though still not hungry, I must be feeling better. For the first time I realise that I haven't been to school this week. I vaguely remember her telling me days ago that Liz and Jenny had been calling. Have they stopped? Do friends lose interest that quickly too?

My heart pounds through my chest as I get a flashback to the last phone call I made. I rang his house the next afternoon and his mum told me he had transferred to Brisbane. She asked me if I knew why he would suddenly up and leave and I just slammed the phone down and cried. Angry tears. Sad tears. Tears of relief and fury. How dare he!

It is possible that the radio has been on all day? Maybe Mum turned it on this morning. Maybe she has been turning it on every morning, but I'm only now tuning in to it.

Meatloaf groans out the rock ballad lyrics, "I want you, I need you. But there ain't no way I'm ever gonna love you. Now don't be sad, 'cause two out of three ain't bad."

I can't imagine a female ever singing those words. In fact, now I wonder what the writer did to make him say it. Did he also rape his girlfriend, take away her virginity and then leave town?

Farewell cases

The left wheel on my suitcase catches in the sheet. It snags as I try to drag it from the bed and turn to say thank you to my favourite nurse at the same time. She believes me that I would never do it again. The shrink didn't, and Mum has made it very clear that she still doesn't.

I was hoping that Troy would be here to pick me up. He told me he would support me. That he wanted this baby too.

Instead, Mum escorts me to the car, oblivious to my need for a hug. Physical touch wasn't allowed in this rehab, 'In fear that bad relationships may form'.

I open the back and lay my suitcase in the carpeted boot. Even from the back of the station wagon, the car smells like my baby girl, a recipe of spew and talcum powder. I open the back door, but the car seat is empty.

'Where is she? Where's Chelsea?'

'Steve's minding her. I thought you'd like a quiet trip home.'

'Mum, I haven't seen her in six weeks …' Her face changes, I've upset her. 'But thank you for thinking of me like that.'

We drive the forty-minute drive in complete silence. I am tired and cranky that I have to wait even longer to see my little girl.

Mum was obviously brooding over my comment. It would have been nice to be welcomed home like a normal person.

As I raise my door handle, Mum reaches out and touches my wrist.

'The social worker will be here at five.' With no time for me to question her, she gets out of the car and rushes inside. I collect my suitcase, and suddenly feel like a stranger about to enter my own home.

Mum is holding Chelsea and Steve completes the little trio family embrace. Neither extends her towards me.

'I was only away for six weeks. You know she's mine, right!'

I lean in to take her, but she no longer knows who I am. She frowns and snuggles deeper into Mum's neck.

Subconsciously, I notice that the room seems empty, but I only have eyes for Chelsea.

Finally, she feels safe enough to allow me to hold her – just as the doorbell rings – and she jumps. We both glance towards the entry and make faces as Mum solemnly invites her guest in.

I hold Chelsea tight, relishing every smile and touch as my baby starts to remember me again.

As I sit, glued cross-legged to the rug, I go numb as Mum explains that Janice is here to discuss the adoption process. The process of taking my baby away. After the police became involved, together they devised this plan. Janice makes an attempt to reassure me: 'We have everyone's best interest at heart. We decided not to mention it while you were in hospital, just in case you couldn't handle it'.

After a long time, I became aware that there were no thoughts running through my head. Nothing. No anger. No sadness. Nothing. I was emotionless. Emotionless, yet fragile. I felt like I would crumble if I even breathed too hard.

As darkness covered the windows and filled the room, Mum turned on the light, and reality blinded me.

'You're right. My little princess deserves a proper family.' I glare at Mum then Steve and finally stand to pass Chelsea to the social worker.

'We'll be back for her and her things tomorrow at ten, dear.'

With the authority gone, Mum relaxes into her true anger.

'I hate the idea of Chelsea going to strangers!' She declares, 'If I can't have her then ...'

'Mum!'

'I don't mean that. I just mean. Well, I can't stay here without her, and I definitely can't be here when they take her away. Steve has asked me to move to Perth with him.'

That's why the house seems empty. They are moving. She's already started packing. I wonder if she even considered the idea of taking me. It's just them now, a couple. And soon it will be just me. No Mum. No baby. Just me.

With one final kiss on the cheek, Mum hands me a piece of blue paper with her new address on it, and turns toward the door. Behind her, Steve drags the big red suitcase out to the car; and they are gone.

With Chelsea in my arms, I wander around to see what wasn't important enough for her to take with her. All the photos and trinkets are still in place. She has really only taken things she can wear: clothes, makeup and jewellery. No reminders of her only daughter. None of her only granddaughter.

At five to ten the social worker arrives to take Chelsea.

After a full night of gauging thoughts, and a new stern protective wall, I take my last chance, hoping she will tell me where Chelsea's father is. 'Do you know where Troy is? He's not returning any of my messages and I haven't seen him since he was arrested. Nobody will tell me anything!'

'He's okay. They released him. Because he was nineteen, but you fell pregnant before you turned eighteen …'

'By two months!'

'I know, but the police had to enforce the law. They placed an AVO on him, so he is not allowed anywhere near you or Chelsea. If he contacts you, he *will* go to jail.'

Niceties over, she returns to business. 'Now, we provide the car seat and her new family …' She sees me cringe. 'They have a nursery set up. But does she have any favourite toys you would like to send with her?'

I point to the little red suitcase near the front door.

'The Salvos will call you tomorrow to arrange a time to collect her other things.'

Good. There's a lot more here they can take too.

With shaking hands, I draw my innocent bundle into my neck for one final embrace. My arms feel so heavy and my legs so weak that I fear I am going to fall. But if I did, it would go on my record that I hurt my own child. No one would believe that it was just the strain of the pain.

She is so small, so precious, so fragile – yet so strong. She smells so pure, unlike me. With numbness from my head to my heart, I carefully step one foot at a time through the doorway where her transporter is waiting to take her to her new mother. Chelsea looks into my eyes and smiles so intentionally. I buckle to the patio pavers, and try to absorb her into my heart through my clothes and skin. To keep her forever. Even just a small part of her.

But no, this is what's best for her. *This isn't about what I want. It's what she needs.* I've recited it so many times in the last fifteen hours that I almost believe it. Believe that this is good for her. Believe that what I want doesn't matter. That I don't matter ... I guess I don't.

The next morning, my aunt rings to welcome me home and ask about Chelsea. I can't bring myself to say the words out loud, so I tell her she's asleep.

The clock says it's lunch time, but I'm still not hungry. I wander around the ghostly house looking for things I want to keep. The middle size red suitcase fits everything with space to spare.

Thankfully, the men from the Salvos were able to come today. I give them everything that had belonged to Chelsea.

Then everything that had belonged to mum.

All the trinkets I had given her, all the photos of us together, all the things that she left behind – all the reminders of family that my mum didn't want.

She didn't take anything to remind her of me or of Chelsea. She has completely left us behind.

Did she ever really love me? Was my whole life was fake?

I gave them everything that I thought had belonged to me. Belonging and ownership are only permanent until they're not. And there's nothing left to matter anymore. Nothing is permanent. Nothing matters any more than I do.

I place the keys and Mum's blue address card into an envelope. This fits into the postal slot of the real estate agent. Not my responsibility.

The wheel of my suitcase gets caught in the gap as I step into the train.

I know I can make good money working nights in Sydney. My clients won't love me, but at least they won't pretend they do.

Belt up

He entered the room and handed me a white plastic bag.

Vinnies thirty cents. The faded price tag was still attached to the plaited leather belt inside.

'Thanks. I love belts.'

Always safer to prevent his embarrassment, I held the tag away from me to pretend I hadn't seen it, and added, 'But look, is this the price tag? Do you want to take it off before I see it?'

He yanked the belt from my hand and broke the price tag string with one snap.

'What I paid for it doesn't matter. The point is, *I* gave it to you, so put it on.' He announced. 'Now!'

With shaky hands I instinctively obeyed. Then, after inspection, he left the room.

As I cleared the breakfast plates and my white plastic birthday wrapping, I caught a glimpse of my husband as he left for work. He had his briefcase in one hand and a garbage bag in the other. *A garbage bag? That's weird. Why is he taking the rubbish out? And why didn't he get the rubbish from this bin? Oh well, I must remember to thank him for that when he calms down.*

Before I could even unlock the front door, I could hear the pure joyous energy in the form of my best friend. Jen was bouncing up and down, crying, 'Happy birthday to you. Happy birthday ...'

My heart joined her in dancing and tears of laughter replaced the stains from those that had escaped earlier. I opened the screen door as I took in the image standing before me. Her arms were overflowing with presents, a huge bunch of helium-filled balloons, and a cake with candles already alight.

I don't know how, but as she entered, she still managed to give me a kiss and a hug. It may have been only a lean in with a forearm bump, and a peck on the cheek, but the love in that moment was more than I had felt in a long time.

Jen made us both a coffee, insisting I was not allowed to do such menial tasks on my birthday. Between laughter, gossip and family updates, we realised it had been eight months since we saw each other. She was such a dutiful wife, following her husband around the country.

Then she handed me my presents one at a time. Drawing out the gift-giving was something we both inflicted on each other year after year. I opened the first two gifts – a leather journal and a mouse for my laptop. Jen gives such perfect presents; she always seems to know both what I want *and* need. I wish she knew everything. Under a mass of shiny ribbons and bows, the third gift contained a cylindrical box. As I removed the lid, I first saw a gold buckle attached to a brown leather belt.

Whack! The impact forced me forward onto the bed where I copped two more across the middle of my back. The intensity of the burning was as real as the original event, and my reflexes sent a shudder through my body.

'Hey,' I heard Jen's voice, 'Are you okay?'

'Yeah, of course. Sorry.' I placed that belt on the table without further comment and reached in for the item below.

The second belt was a beautiful woven cotton creation of plaited ribbons with dangling tassels. 'Ooh, this is sooo pretty!'

I immediately stood up and replaced the belt I had received earlier that morning with this new one. It didn't matter that it totally clashed with my shirt. A happy twirl landed me uncoordinated back onto my seat. We both laughed.

Pulling out the third belt, I squealed with delight.

'Oh Jen! Where on earth did you find this? It's perfect. Thank you soooo much!'

'It should be. It's the one you described on Facebook two weeks ago.' She laughed with mock indignance.

I jumped up again, hugged her tight and then pulled her to her feet.

'Come and look. You've got to see the skirt I want to wear it with.'

Arm in arm like two teenage girls, my best friend and I tottered up the hallway, playfully bumping each other into walls and doorframes. I urgently wanted to show her my early birthday present from Mum – the pinstripe skirt that needed this precise belt. Sliding open the wardrobe door, my hand hesitated when I heard a car door. Then panic struck.

My heart stopped and started again with a jolt. I threw the perfect belt onto the bed and ran back to the dining room to get the one I was supposed to be wearing. The belt *he* had given me. I struggled to untie the ribbon belt, my fingers knotted in the tassels and loops, mixed with sweaty palms. Hoping to look inconspicuous, I re-entered the bedroom with the proper belt almost completely looped.

Jen was still standing at the wardrobe door where I had left her. Staring at me, this conversation could go one of two ways. I could pretend to be the loving wife, wanting to please her husband, or tell her the truth and release the pent-up tears. The latter wasn't an option if that car door was his.

Best to pretend the last moment hadn't happened. Besides, it was only the neighbour.

I picked up the prized belt from the bed and reached into the wardrobe. Knowing the exact order of every item in the cupboard, it was easy to find the skirt and pull it out. I held it against my waist, and dangled my new belt over it.

Before I looked up, I explained, 'See, this is the exact size for these big loops, and it matches the blue line perfectly.' With a swish, I looked up at her proudly, ready to reveal the perfect coordination. Jen was rigid. Her eyes were fixed on my belt rack at the other end of the wardrobe.

'Tash,' she stammered. Where are all your other belts?'

I spun round.

The belts were gone. I yanked my dresses and skirts back and forth. This had to be a mistake, a joke. Sixty belts – gone.

N.B. For readers who may think this story is contradictory, please know that there is a human determination that makes victims learn to overcome, and even love, those things that have had dominance over them. This can be sex, hunger, pain or, in this case, belts.

Drunk as
a hoot

Drunk as a hoot owl, writing letters by thunderstorm.

That's the text that Dad received at 2:14 am.

Oh shoot. I told Mum I'd be home by nine. Damn Trudy. Why'd she need me to go to her place tonight? She musta known I'd get lost trying to get home again. I've never been from the pub to her house then to my house before. It's confusing. And it's dark. And, oh great, now it's raining.

'M'am. 'scuse me m'am. Can you please tell me what time it is? I gotta be home by ten.'

'Well I'm afraid you're late dear, it's twelve-thirty.'

'Bugger. Oops, sorry! I don't meana swear in fron' of a lady. Sorry.'

Oh good, that pub's open. Maybe they've got a phone and I can call Mum. Tell her I'm on my way.

'Hi. Hi. Do you's 'ave a phone I can use? Please. I meant to say dat firs', sorry. Do you's *please* 'ave a phone?'

'Sorry young lady. You've had too much to drink. I cannot let you enter these premises.'

'I haven' been … oh, okay … maybe I 'ave. But I don't wanna drink. I just needsa use ya phone.'

'Go home young lady.'

'I. Am. Trying! But I'm late.'

He unfolds his big arms. Man they're big. And points down the street.

'But! Wait! Wait! If ya won't le' me use ya phone, have ya got a bit of paper I can have? Oh, an' a pen? Please. Please can I have a pen.'

'Why?' Nosey security guy.

'I needsa le' me mumma know I's alright.'

Nosey security guy pulled out his radio thingy and asked someone to bring some paper and a pen to 'Door Number One'.

When the lady arrived with it, he just pointed to me. She gave it to me and he, once again, told me to leave. Mean security guy.

Dis is good. I can't find home. They won't let me phone home. Ha ha. ET phone home. Dat's really funny! Um … yeah … I can't phone mum so I will write her a ledda.

I sit down on the seat in a taxi stand near the beach and start writing.

Dear Mum,

I ~~sorry~~ am sorry I am late. I am to trying get home but I is lost.

See yoo soon xo

I betta tell dad too, cos he's at work so he won' know I'm not home yet too.

~~Dar~~ Dear Dad

I told Mum already. I am lost. Home soon.

Hope fun at work,

The rain is getting heavier and the lightning and thunder have started.

I bes' move unda outa da rain or the paper'll ged wet. So I walk across the sand to the jetty and crouch underneath.

'Hey Mis'er Fish! Mis'er Fish, I wanna as' you a queshun. If dat lightnin' gets … closer, is it safer or more dangerouser unda dis bridge?'

Stupid fish. Just cos he's safe in the water. He should still answer me to help me be safe too. Oh well. The paper's getting' wet anyway, so I will go under the bridge. Just so the lightning doesn't make the paper any wetter.

'Hey Mis'er Fish! I finish me ledders now so I goin' home. Okay? Is dat okay?'

It seems to take forever to cross the beach, then cross the road, then walk past Mary's place and up my four front steps.

'Where on earth have you been?' Mum asks really loudly. 'It's pouring! Your father and I have been worried sick!'

'But I told you. Here ... I wrote you leddas.' I hand her the letters and ...

The next morning dad shows me the last texts between he and mum.

Steve (2:13am)   Any news? Is she home yet? What on earth is she doing?

Pat (2:14am)   Yes ... Drunk as a hoot owl, writing letters by thunderstorm.

Don't let them see

This story was first published in Beneath the Surface in 2020.

One day at a time. That's what they all say. Just one day at a time.

The psychiatrist had explained that the waves come in twenty-minute cycles. So one day is a long time. In fact, that's seventy-two cycles to endure.

Every. Single. Day. That's seventy-two opportunities to succeed or fail. That's seventy-two tests to pass. That's seventy-two times to doubt, question, and torture yourself. *Seventy-two* times to hide it from the world.

Every day. Every single day.

Will this ever end. Is this really worth it anyway?

Yes!

Or so they say.

It's 6:13 and the kids will wake soon. Good mums are up before their kids, so it's time to get out of bed.

Ashleigh on the bus at 8:40.

Bella to playgroup at 9:00.

John to TAFE at 9:30.

Home by 9:50.

Then what?

Focus, woman, focus! I tell myself and I put one foot deliberately onto the floor. Today I will not drink. Today I will survive. They will not know how I really feel. And I will look normal.

Two feet on the floor. Shoulders back. Dressing gown on. You've got this.

Ashleigh is the first one awake. She meets me in the kitchen as I pour the water into my coffee.

'Hi darling.' The words sound jittery, but I don't think she notices. Try again. 'What's on today? Anything special?'

'Nah,' she offers, 'Just another dumb test.'

'Why …' I start to ask why she didn't tell me, but maybe she did.

I can't appear to have forgotten yet another school event. 'Why is it dumb?' Nice recovery woman!

After a while, Bella wanders out and I let her wake up properly before offering her a hug. She is the least affectionate of the three, probably because touch is something she has had very little of. Life has many phases and the children are always the victims.

I have to wake John for TAFE. He chose to become a carpenter and I am so proud of him, but teenagers seem to need more sleep than any other age group. I sit gently on the edge of his bed and just look at his face. Oh, the hurt he has suffered. The pain he has felt.

I am so sorry my darling. If I could take it all back, I would. You are so strong and so mature, but for all the wrong reasons. I am so sorry. I wish I could go back to when it was just you and me. We were a great team. My best mate. John, I love you so much.

Part of me is tempted to let him sleep. To stay in his paradise free from reality, but I know he wants to go to TAFE. After all, his apprenticeship is his ticket to freedom. With that he has a title, a purpose, an income, a career. A reason to live. And a means of escape.

I yell at myself. It was not all my fault! Now shut up and put on the brave face. You've got this.

'Wakey wakey, rise and shine. Come on Johnno, it's getting up time.' That's been his alarm since he was less than a year old.

When I return to the kitchen, with the promise that John will be there soon, Ashleigh is already making toast and has the cereal and milk on the table. I watch with sadness at the capability of one so young. This five-year-old is as familiar in the kitchen as I am, maybe more so – and not because I was such a great mum that I taught her. No, when you're hungry and your dad's nowhere around and your mother is drunk, you learn to fend for yourself.

She'll go far. She will succeed at anything she does. She is so capable. But I want her to have a childhood. I want her to play and laugh. But no, she's too busy being mum to her siblings. I'm grateful to her and angry at myself for this situation.

The tears well. I hate myself for causing my kids to grow up so fast. They're so young. Stop it! Get a grip! It's 7:45 so you can collapse in two hours and five minutes. Not now. Not in front of them. They don't need to pick you up again.

'Ashleigh, look at you darling. You are amazing! What can I do to help? Would you like me to get the plates? Butter the toast? Thank you so much for making breakfast.' And I lean in to hug her.

'No, Mum. It's fine.'

As I open the cupboard door to retrieve bowls, plates and glasses, my eyes are drawn to one item only. That glass. Everything else is opaque, but that one glass is crystal clear. The wave is back. That glass is the perfect size and shape for a double shot of bourbon, two ice cubes and just the right amount of coke. That glass has survived many a fun time. Others have broken but that one remains. My friend. Stop it. It's just a glass. In fact, if it's a problem, get rid of it. I can't throw it out now though, Ashleigh would see me do that and know I have a problem. I don't have a problem. I'm sober. It's just a glass.

I steadily take four plates and bowls to the table. Then I turn back for the cutlery but notice Ashleigh has them in one hand and the buttered toast in the other. Did I just lose time again or does she work really fast?

'Sorry, darling. I was going to do that for you.'

'It's okay, Mum. Stop stressing.'

That's my cue to shut up, so I smile on the outside and kick myself on the inside. I will not let her see the tears. I will not.

Even from the driveway, the house always seems the quietest when I arrive back after the morning school run. As I pause to look, the old rush of excitement returns – six hours until they're home. That's three hours to drink, two to sleep and sober up, one to shower and wake up before I go and get them. It's a routine I know well.

Not today. Not any more. I hope. That's the plan.

One day at a time.

Today is a new day. Today I have a new plan. One hour of cleaning, then one hour of reading. Lunch, phone my sister, then watch a DVD.

Nothing major, nothing stressful. One day my life will be useful again, but for now I survive.

The next time I look at the clock it tells me it's 11:15 – time for another coffee. While the water boils I review my morning achievements. Washing up done. Washing on. Beds made. That was a very productive hour, well done me!

I sit down with my book and coffee and feel the wave again. The second mouthful of coffee tastes like bourbon mixed with diet Pepsi, yuk. Now I know my taste buds are still out of whack.

When the phone rings I am surprised to see the caller is my niece, Karen.

'Hey Kaz, how are you?'

'I … I … Pete's …'

I know the voice. I know the history. I don't need any more information.

'Where are you? I'm on my way!'

'Thank. You. Um … the Alby, room twelve.'

'Don't move.'

I leave my coffee and book where they are, grab my bag and head to the Albion Hotel to help my niece. At least that drunk hasn't put her in hospital again. I only hope I can convince her to leave him *this* time.

Like always, Kaz is restless as she slides through the phases of anger, hurt and guilt. I watch from my seat on the bed, assessing the limp, the welts and the bruises as each of her movements reveals another place his fist connected.

Our words are the same as so many times before, but I hear myself being more forceful now. Not because the assault was any worse, not because I thought there was more chance of her staying away. No, this time, for the first time, I am seeing the situation through sober eyes and I know, I now believe, that there is life without alcohol.

Just then, the motherly instinct kicks in, and I check my watch for the first time since we started talking. It's 2:40 and there is no way I can get to the school in time, and no way I want to leave Karen without her promising to leave Pete for real.

I call my neighbour and ask her to pick up the kids. She knows Karen, so I don't have to say too much before she understands the situation. 'Oh, and my phone is dying, so if you need me we are at the Alby, room twelve.'

Kids safe, I can focus on Karen again.

'I'm starving, can we go get some lunch?'

'Sure,' I reply, 'My shout. Where do you wanna go?'

'Downstairs? Toby still makes great burgers.'

Downstairs. In the restaurant. Attached to the bar.

No problem, I can do this. This is about Karen, not me. I'm sober.

I'm fine. I had been so focussed on her that I actually forgot I was in a pub.

Like clockwork, the temptation flows every twenty minutes. The iced glasses, the bourbons disguised as coke, the wines and beers. NO!

I don't know this cashier, but I order two burgers and add a plate of chips to share. While my back is turned, Karen wanders over to the bar and returns with two drinks – a beer for her and a bourbon and coke for me.

I cannot count the messages flying through my head right now. You can't offend her. Just say no. This is about her. You've got this. One won't matter. Oh I can almost taste the sweetness, the heat …

'Thanks Kaz, but I'm not drinking any more. I'll just have water.'

I did it. I actually said no to a drink! So proud!

To my surprise, Karen doesn't make a big deal out of it. Maybe in a different situation she would have, but today she is too upset and distracted to really notice. She takes it back to the bar – I'm not sure what they do with it, I've never *returned* a drink before.

As we finished our lunch, the waiter comes and clears out plates.

'Hi Joy, you had a phone call.'

I start to stand, quickly assuming it is my neighbour, and something is wrong with the kids.

His hand goes out to stop me. 'No, it's ok, he hung up.'

My puzzled frown invites more information.

'Your son, John, rang and asked if you were here. I started to say, "Yeah hang on mate, I'll get her." But he hung up.'

My mouth drops to my heart. My heart drops to my stomach.

I'm at a pub and the kids know. No matter what they're told, they will assume I'm drinking.

I have to get home.

They have to see that I didn't drink.

'Karen, I am *really* sorry but I *have* to go.'

That too, was easier than I expected.

'Can I come with you?'

'Of course! But we have to go *now*. Are you getting your stuff or coming back here?'

We race up to her room, but time seems to be in slow motion as we throw her few belongings into her overnight bag.

I am desperate to see my kids. For them to see me. Sober.

Checking out takes forever. Driving takes forever. Reaching my kids takes forever.

When I open that front door and see the three of them huddled on the lounge, John reading to his younger sisters, my heart stops. They all look up, not with excitement, but with the familiar terror – expecting me to stagger in drunk. But this time I'm sober.

John was the first to meet my eyes and his head did a double take as he realised that I wasn't drunk.

Tears fall as I watch him slowly remove his arms from Ashleigh and Bella's shoulders and say 'Mummy's home'.

He walks cautiously toward me without taking his eyes from mine. The smile on both our faces grows as he approaches.

'Thank you. I couldn't be prouder. You've got this mum. I love you so much.'

Here we go again

This story won third place in the Odyssey House Competition in 2019 and was published on their website.

The house is in a silent mood. It breathes life, but it sobs quietly.

My best friend laughed at me when I tried to explain this, but maybe normal houses don't act the same as ours.

I know its moods. I can tell when it's empty. I can tell when she's in there, passed out. Even then, there are two moods – music blaring, hiding the real noises; or silent and regular whirs of household machinery, the survival mode of the place we call home.

Today the house cries. The regular heartbeats can be heard.

Today is her payday so Mum will be lying on the lounge, trying to recover from her morning's binge. The edge of the 750ml Jim Beam bottle on the floor, leans against a cushion she would have carefully placed on her way to oblivion.

She does weird stuff like that, she thinks she's so clever while having no idea how stupid it is to need a cushion to stop your bourbon from spilling. Just stand it up. Or. Don't. Drink.

Tuesdays are the worst, as she runs out of money and the withdrawals kick in.

'I need to *go bush*,' she tells me with a determination that is only disguised by misery.

Is this the time? Will she come home this time? Should I call the police again? Will the 'incident' be an accident or deliberate; serious, embarrassing or fatal?

She tells us she loves us, but I know she wants out. Why aren't we enough? Why can't she just choose us and stay?

How much planning she puts into it shows how serious she is, how hurt she is and the likelihood of her returning safely. *Going bush* is her way of escaping, her solitude – and it will either refresh her or give her the means to injure herself – accidentally or carelessly.

Either way, it's a waiting game to see if she comes home, in what condition, by what mode – police, ambulance or taxi after the stay in hospital. And I know, one day, she won't.

I hate this.

The thoughts that terrify me are those when I wish it was over. And it's not that I want her dead. It's not that I want her out of my life. I love my mum. I just wish this rollercoaster would stop. When she's well she's a loving mum, hard-working but always there for the three of us. When she's depressed, or on a drinking binge, she's ... a burden.

She hates it too, I know. But she gets to escape by drinking herself into unconsciousness or by going bush, or by talking to her therapists.

I don't get to escape. I live with the constant fear, walking up that driveway – what mood will the house be in today. I jump whenever the phone rings – it could be the police or the hospital. I can't plan to go out with my friends, just in case she needs me. And none of us have brought friends to the house since Dad died.

What will my role be today? Will I be playing mum, housekeeper or counsellor? I hate having to play doctor. Seeing her bleed makes me want to vomit. Seeing her vomit makes me want to scream.

I am always first home. My brother finishes work later than we girls finish school – lucky him. My little sister finishes at the same time as me, but her bus route takes her around town, so she arrives home about twenty-five minutes after me.

I could dawdle, and we could both enter the house together, but there are sights I never want in her head. That's why I leave my last class ten minutes early and race home – to fix up the worst of it before she enters the house.

As I push the key into the lock, I glance to see who's turning into the driveway. Oh great. Mum must have been drunk-texting again, and here's the Pastor to check on her.

'Hi Stacey, how are you? You haven't been inside yet?' He glances down at the key in the door.

'Nope, just got home.' I state the obvious, trying not to be sarcastic.

'How about you wait out here while I go check on ya mum?'

'It's okay Pastor Steve, I think I know why you're here.'

'Stacey, this is adult stuff. Let me deal with it, okay. You couldn't understand.'

With a roll of my eyes, I remove the key from the now unlocked door and push it open. Without moving, I sweep my right arm through the doorway, inviting him into my house that I am not welcome in. 'Please, go on in,' I tell him.

Oh, how I wish it could be *adult stuff* – then I wouldn't have to deal with it! But I do. This is my lot in life, regardless of my age. At thirteen, I have no doubt seen more than he has in his entire lifetime.

After twenty minutes of no return, I assume Mum is in her argumentative mood, fighting his every suggestion.

He'll try, 'Why don't you have a cuppa?' and she'll reply, 'Why don't you rack off!'

He'll suggest, 'Why don't you try and sleep it off?' and she'll yell, 'Leave me alone, I don't need sleep!'

I pull out my homework and try to concentrate on something other than the house. It obviously works, I don't hear him return.

'Your mum is watching TV. Be a good girl. Try to let her rest. She's under a lot of stress so try to see things from her view. I'll have someone send something over for dinner and I'll check on her tomorrow.'

And with a sympathetic – condescending – pat on the shoulder he leaves, just as I hear Mel's bus coming around the corner.

Yet another 'Knight in Shining Armour' comes bounding in and *saves the day* … and leaves.

He gets to drive away. He gets to come and go. Jeez, even Mum gets to come and go as she pleases. I don't.

And he will have someone bring over a meal! What's with that? Who the hell does he think cooks every other meal on every other day when she *doesn't* drunk-text someone? Who does he think looks after everyone and does the housework?

And don't tell me *she's* stressed. She's a drunk. A useless drunk!

'Hey sis, why ya sittin' out here?' Chirpy Mel bounces up the driveway, pausing on her way. 'Just enjoying the fresh air while I wait for you.' I reply, faking a smile. 'Good day?'

'Pretty cool. Our table won the Best Table Award and 'cos I have the most merit points, I got to pick the first prize and Miss Archer said there was something special in the box this week and *I picked it out*! Look, it's a Best Friends Forever necklace and it's all mine.'

She holds up the silver crescent around her neck and I read it aloud, 'Best For'.

She is so excited that I instantly forget about the house and its mood, and Mum. This is what life after school *should* be like.

'Stacey,' she eases closer, reaching into her pocket, then holds her hand out to me, 'I want you to have the other half.'

She hands me the pendant and I read it to her, adding, 'That's what we are, 'Friends Ever'. Best friends for ever.'

'I know.'

We hug and she skips toward the house.

I automatically react to stop her but know that Pastor Steve would have done the *adult thing* and tidied up like always. Mel can just walk in and see Mum watching TV, at least sober enough to disguise her day's events from one so young.

So, I stay outside for a while, looking at my new necklace with its half-heart shape and inscription.

This is just like Mum, half a heart. Broken in two. Two halves that make a whole, but not complete. I love one part and want to keep it close to my heart, but the other half is distant and disconnected from me. I only ever have one half of my Mum's love.

Something inside me smiles at this thought.

'You know what,' I say aloud without caring if neighbours can hear, 'I love you Mum, so that's the half I'm going to focus on.'

With this new picture in my head and my new pendant around my neck, I stand up and face the house.

'Hi darling,' she stammers as I enter the loungeroom. Her eyes quickly give me the routine line of how sorry she is, followed by the request to please keep this a secret. 'How was school?'

'Hmm, not bad. I gave it a *half-hearted* attempt.' I raise the pendant, smile on the inside and wink at Mel. As I make myself comfortable on the lounge with them, Mel continues telling Mum about her day. I then realise that the mood has lightened. The house has wiped away today's tears.

Driving lessons

From the time Tony challenged me to a drag through Singleton and The Heights, I was never going to let a man beat me behind the wheel of a car.

My brother is probably responsible for injecting the need for speed into my veins. He was always tinkering on one vehicle or another and the police were always bringing him home for breaking some kind of road rule – the most common being Driving Without a Licence.

In the years since I obtained my licence, I have accepted multiple challenges. Sitting at a red light, it only takes a raised chin, slight tilt then a slow nod to indicate that it's on once the colour changes.

My first car was a Torana and, just like a horse where rider and animal instinctively know the powers and weaknesses of the other, my car and I knew each other well.

I never lost.

I also never received a fine and I never had an accident – well, none that were my fault.

Behind the wheel, my life has been a series of fortunate events.

I upgraded cars every couple of years – sometimes to remain inconspicuous, sometimes I thought it was time to 'grow up', other times I just wanted more power. But no matter the car, I always won.

Sure, I would back off the accelerator when I suspected the presence of the cops, or I knew the car didn't like the gradient of a particular corner, but it was on as soon as the risk was in the mirror. And, undoubtedly, my competitor failed to calculate their risks in advance so I would catch up and pass them – usually on the side of the road in front of a police car or in a ditch.

Then one day something happened. I was stopped at the lights with a solo male in the car beside me. The chin, the tilt, then the nod – and we were off.

But this guy was too enthusiastic, he looked like he has never had a win in his life and he was desperate to prove his masculinity. I hit the accelerator and changed up – first, second, third – then took my time slowly moving to fourth, still watching the grin on his face.

He needed this. His ego needed to win. And who was I to let a ninety-year-old fail in the prime of his life.

I maintained the speed limit – another rare occurrence for me – and let him claim his victory as we approached the next set of lights and slowed at the amber.

He won. I lost. A victory for both.

Supping above the canopy

The need to 'go bush' always coincides with my need to leave my real life. It's a practice reserved for when I can no longer stand the busy-ness anymore – or the chaos, the sadness, or pain.

To me, the bush is peace. Freedom. Serenity. My way of escaping the world that I am otherwise lost in.

Thursday's destination was a property my parents used to own. The house was long-gone, but I knew the dirt tracks and dam were still there. By leaving my car outside the gate and climbing the fence, I could justify to myself that I was not breaking and entering; I was purely visiting an old home.

The first paddock was open, with dirt tracks made by vehicles so frequent that the weeds could no longer grow on them. Eucalyptus and gum trees framed the border. I used to listen to the running creek from this spot – now there was only mooing from the neighbours' cows.

Through the creek bed and beyond, where the house once sat, the double tyre tracks became one dirt road – if you can call it a road. It's a compacted dirt path, not quite wide enough for a tractor, not quite smooth enough for bare feet.

I held my right arm up in front of me, bent at a ninety-degree angle, to break any cobwebs before they hit my face. My left arm pushed the spiky branches aside before they could jab me. I kept an eagle eye out for the old mother-in-law prickles that penetrate every item of clothing – best avoided where possible.

The sun's light was now speckled as the canopy thickened above. It matched my moods of late: sometimes bright and other times hidden to the view of others. The canopy, like my solitude, kept me from the strength of the sun.

I feared I have lost them both now.

Joe had to leave town, so he left the state. I thought we would marry one day, but that wasn't meant to be – obviously. His departure was just the beginning. Because of our relationship, I had to leave my church family. Because I lost my church family, as a new Christian I was in danger of losing my close relationship with God. And I loved him too much for that.

'God, where are you?' I asked for the millionth time. I knew he could hear me even when my words were silent. 'Why do you feel so far away when I need you the most?'

The tears fell and I was suddenly weary. In the clearing of another paddock, I clambered up the side of the dam wall and found a place without too many stones or thorns – and sat.

'God, in the Old Testament, you gave people signs. Well now it's my turn. I need a sign! I need a sign that you still love me. Remember the water from the rocks and the wet fleece? I need something visible.'

As the sun disappeared behind a cloud, my mood dulled deeper, and I felt like the earth was putting a barrier between God and me.

'God! I *need* you! Please. I need a miracle. You are my husband, my friend, my brother, my saviour. I need you to come and ... and sit beside me. Let me see you and hold your hand. God *please*, be here with me.'

I turned my head to look at the dirt where I, a mere mortal, expected Jesus to suddenly appear. Nothing.

With both a thirsty heart and mouth, I gave up and resigned myself to losing my man and my God.

I stood and started for home.

To God, our home is in heaven, not here on earth. This place is just temporary. And he has been here in the flesh once – why would he want to go through that again, just because *I* want him to. He could provide an angel at any time, but Jesus was not going to come and sit beside me on that dam wall.

Instead, he drew me to him.

Jesus never leaves, and he certainly never stops loving. It is us who have the short memory and attention span.

My tired sobbing body made it off the dam wall and slumped through the clearing towards the trees. I submerged beneath the canopy and felt the sunlight streaming through like it hadn't done on the journey in.

Suddenly, I was no longer seeing the trees and the path ahead. I was not seeing the world of my body. I was in heaven. My spirit was in heaven!

I don't know whether it was a house or a castle. It felt like an old coffee shop booth. I was inside but I couldn't make out the walls. There was light, and other beings, but I couldn't say who or what they were.

Then he appeared. With a small table between us, my saviour Jesus was sitting across from me. Reachable. Touchable. Real. He pointed to the drink that had appeared before me and I raised the cup and sipped. He did the same. It could have been water, tea or wine; I have no idea. But, like Sunday communion, I was supping with Jesus.

He spoke with a tone so soft. Oral perfection. Though my human mind has never been able to recall most of the words, there is one phrase that I will never forget.

He turned to his right and peered down.

'Look,' he gently told me. 'There you are.'

I looked and saw the human me walking on the path beneath the canopy of trees.

Our eyes met again, and he pointed to the me below.

'It's because you were what you were,' and he nodded at the me opposite him in heaven, 'That you are what you are'.

And with that, our time was over.

I was back walking on the path. A new me.

I tried to recall the entire event. But I couldn't. I longed for the ability to paint so I could capture it and share this miracle with the world, but I can't even draw.

It's because you were what you were, that you are what you are.

The only words I can recall. It's because of who I am on this earth, that makes me the person who will, one day, sit above the canopy and sup with Jesus in heaven.

Jesus wants to have a relationship with us. The difference is that he knows *exactly* what we each need. I didn't need to see him on that dam wall. I needed him to reassure me that, yes, I will stuff up during my time on earth, but one day I will reside with him in heaven.

It was a surreal experience. Some don't believe it was real. But I know it was. Because I have never doubted my salvation since.

The sun was warm on my skin as I danced through the final paddock towards my car. The Son was even warmer within my heart.

Where was I going now? To heaven – via a temporary stopover in my human life.

The case against short platforms

The next stop is Morisset. Morisset next stop.

'Hi darling.' I speak in whispers, the phone jammed against one ear and a finger jammed in the other. 'Are you sure your suit will fit in this suitcase?'

'Yeah. Jake got his mum to do the same thing when he was working FIFO. Same sizes.' My son sounds a lot more confident than I feel. Of course, he doesn't know about the surprise gift that his wife-to-be has asked me to bring down this trip. 'Where are you now?'

'Just waiting to get off. I can't believe my baby's getting married tomorrow.'

I can hear him look at his watch. 'They open at nine, so I should be able to get it and catch the very next train. All going well I'll even get a chance for a shower at your place before the rehearsal dinner.'

'Phew,' he laughs, 'That's ...'

Passengers, please be advised that Morisset is a short platform. You must exit the train from one of the last four carriages.

Mid-conversation it hits me. This train has eight carriages and I got in the front one. I can't exit from here!

Panic strikes. I hope Rob can hear as I call, 'Gotta go...' while lowering my phone to my side. No time to find the end button. I grab my suitcase and open the internal carriage door. *Of course, it's the old train with manual internal doors.* Through the connection area and another manual door. This area is barely big enough for me and this old bag.

Into the next carriage. There's a group of people on the right with their arms and luggage sprawled over into the aisle. *Why now?* I heave my bag up and over, but the wheel connects with something and throws me to the other side. *More precious microseconds wasted.*

Expletives are shared.

I see out the window that the train is slowing but still no platform in sight. Good.

I straighten the suitcase, and subconsciously make the decision to carry it rather than to try and direct it on its useless wheels.

My pace seems to slow with the train. My feet are tripping over themselves. The stupid bag is banging into every armrest and every arm that dares to still be in its way. But I'm nearly at the door, the end of another carriage. *I'm coming!*

The toe of my sandal folds. The engine of the train fades. I stumble. The train jolts. This stupid travel case hits another *something.*

The breaks screech as they slow the train. I squeal as my travels come to a sudden halt on the floor. The train has stopped. I am stopped.

Then, with every iota of determination, I untangle myself from that hunk of junk and throw us both through the next two connection area doors.

I see glass. I see the platform. I see…

Stand clear. Doors closing.

Tosser child

As I stand among the growing crowd on platform twenty-three, I visualise the draft outline of the Criminology essay that's due on Sunday. I need to finish it today, so I hope for a single seat in a quiet carriage.

The 12:40 from Central Station is always busy, but tottering along the narrow aisles I find a vacant double seat in the fifth carriage, a Quiet Carriage.

After sliding across to the window seat, I open my bag while scanning the passengers, glad to see most have books in their hands or headphones in their ears.

This may be a quiet trip after all.

The train is already slowing for the next station and I sigh as I wait for my laptop to load, frustrated at every wasted moment, knowing I only have three hours to finish this assessment.

I stare intently at my laptop as the new passengers rush to find their seats, hoping they all realise that I am not to be interrupted, holding my breath in anticipation until they are all seated and I can focus again.

'Mummy, it landed on top of the train,' a little boy of about four tells his distracted parent.

'Yes, that's very clever darling.' She answers, from rote rather than interest.

Forgetting about my work, my mind is suddenly racing with fear and rage. Are you kidding? That's not very clever. That's very dangerous!

I can't believe no-one else cares about this. Just what did this kid throw that landed on top of the train? If it was metallic, we could all end up electrocuted. If it's sharp, it's going to fly off and hurt someone. What if it's alive? What is it? Should I ask him? Should I tell the guard?

No, I need to get this essay done. Someone else will take care of it.

I am 980 words into my first draft when something catches my eye. Two rows ahead, on the opposite side of the aisle, something is seeping down the outside of the window. Not flooding, just constant. Dark red in places, almost black in others.

We've been travelling for about twenty minutes. Long enough for that tosser's missile to do its damage.

Is it oil? What's leaking? What was broken?

Is it blood? I need to tell the guard. Now!

If only I was sitting closer. Why hasn't that couple seen it? Wake up. Take your headphones off. Look at your window. There's something on the roof that is dangerous or injured.

This is serious. More important than my essay.

I slam my laptop shut, shove it into its carry-bag and ram that into my backpack. Moving as quickly as I can, I stand, swing the backpack through one arm, around my back, and insert my other arm.

My steps are heavy and deliberate as I step out into the aisle – heading for the guard's office at the front of the train. Passing through the vestibule, that vandal child and his mother are waiting to depart at the next station.

'Mummy, now can I get my ice-cream off the roof?'

Reasons to live

The pendant around my neck reminds me daily with its inscription, *Reasons to live*.

For nearly fifteen years, I struggled to stay alive. My only motive was to see my children all aged over twenty-one which – in my warped mind – meant they wouldn't need me anymore.

I would be free to end my life.

I related innately to Robin Williams – the world knew him as a comedian, but it wasn't until after his death that it was revealed he had suffered from an inner torment that shredded him apart on a regular basis.

Some call it mental illness. Some say it's the way of the creative's mind. Others blame a spiritual, physical or other imbalance of health. I say it's torture. A hidden torture that you cannot share with the world.

Until recently.

In modern times, people are encouraged to share their anxieties and stresses.

Sadly, this had led to a lot of people becoming intolerant and weak. When your cat dies you are sad, you are not suffering from depression. When you get butterflies or feel nauseous before doing a speech, you are nervous not suffering from anxiety. These things are normal. They are a part of the adrenalin that motivates us human beings. They even protect us in dangerous circumstances.

They are *not* mental illness.

Did I have reasons to live? I had three – Rob, Jess and Kelly.

Could they live without me? I believed they would be better off without me. To exit their world would be a gift to them. That's mental illness. That's a warped mind that reality cannot fix.

In a similar fashion, let's look at body image. Most females don't like the way they look. Many dislike having their photo taken. That's a normal circumstance of the pressure society has put on us and the expectations we have conjured up in our minds.

Those suffering from eating disorders such as Anorexia Nervosa have this in common — but it goes a step deeper. When they look in the mirror or down at their body, they actually see it differently to how others see it. They wear distorted glasses, calculations are made with a distorted formula in their mind as to what is normal, fat, ugly … and, I can tell you from personal experience, that this does not go away.

Even when you eat 'normally', your image of yourself still differs. You eat but always critique its fat value and the guilt of knowing that you can do without this, that you'd be better off without this. These thoughts quickly become 'You're weak for eating this, you know better, you don't need this, this will make you fat'.

There is never a break. And the world around you carries on unaware of all of it.

They only notice when, in *their* eyes, you look too skinny.

Just like they only notice when, in *their* eyes, you behave too irrationally.

Did I have reasons to live? Of course I did. Were they enough to make me want to live? Only my children were — and yet I believed they would be better off without me, which negated the only reasons I had.

Evidence

Her car collided with the tree. It wasn't a suicide attempt. She just didn't have the mental capacity to stop it.

His car collided with the gutter. It wasn't careless or reckless. He was just excited, now able to sign the affidavit to get the children taken from her.

She cried every night when she couldn't tuck her babies into bed.

He yelled every night when they didn't drift into slumber quickly enough.

She wasn't given the court notice which would have allowed her to get her paperwork together.

He withheld the documents, choosing instead to maintain the control he'd held for almost a decade.

The sympathetic judge saw that she was unprepared, and glared at the lawyer, for he knew he could make decisions based only on the evidence submitted.

The man knew this in advance.

The woman learned of this in the courtroom.

His testimony told the court she was intending to kill herself and their children. She was now considered a risk and was terrified of losing them permanently.

The man left with temporary custody of the children. He didn't want them, but didn't want her to win.

The woman left with weekly supervised visits. She didn't need watching but would take any time she could get.

She now has days to fill between visits. Days contain hours and hours contain minutes. Even a second takes forever when your children are not allowed to be with you.

She prepares her evidence, attends the meetings, does all the right things – to prove to the judge that she is the better parent.

In the lonely nights, she sums up her life as nothingness.

She has no car – it was written off in the accident. She has no job prospects – she's always been a stay-at-home mum to her two children.

She has no income – her Parenting Payment stopped because she doesn't have the children now.

She has no rent – the eviction notice arrived yesterday.

She is trying to hold the Real Estate off until after court, she cannot have the children without a home. She has no food – the crisis support has ended.

She has no children most of the time – they are with her ex-husband and his new girlfriend.

She has nothing to make her happy – except the nightly phone call with her children and the sparse weekend hours together.

Judgement day finally arrives. Today her Legal Aid lawyer gets to tell the judge all the reasons why the children should be with the mother and not the father. Today her life becomes full again, nothingness becomes history.

An early start, coffee in hand, her mother drives her to Parramatta Court to get the verdict. She has started driving again, but today she doesn't want to think about anything but getting her babies back.

The lights change. The man speeds. The woman screams. The car...

Today, the father goes home with full-time custody.

Today the father learns that if he hadn't lied in the first place, the mother of his children would not have been on her way to court.

Waking for adventure

This child could sleep through anything!

Being raised among the clamour of an inner city, my five-year-old grandson is immune to noise. From the day they came home from hospital, his mum would vacuum while he slept, tell guests not to speak quietly, and encourage him to fall asleep in various beds.

It's not that my daughter-in-law is selfish or just doesn't want to deal with a difficult sleeper. Rather, she is a brilliant mother who takes every opportunity to train her child in the best ways known. He is the only child I know that asked for Sushi and Brussel Sprouts at three, and truly enjoyed eating them.

This is his first sleepover at Nan and Pop's farm without his parents, and he is loving it. We had so much fun yesterday – wandering the paddocks, tossing stones into the creek, finding the ripe fruit in the orchard, and feeding the animals.

More than just the curiosity of youth, he has a fascination for any – and every – living creature. Big or small, he wants to watch them, touch them, understand and befriend them.

Last night we listened to the nightlife, and studied the stars and the sparkles of a bonfire. After the sunshine, fresh air and exercise that even a sporty city life cannot provide, he fell asleep on Pop's lap bathed in the warmth of his immediate surroundings.

He usually wakes between 6:30 and 7:00 so I take my coffee into his room at 6:20 and simply watch him sleep.

I can't help but smile, reminiscing over the events of yesterday, as I eagerly wait for him to wake up. I cheat a little by opening the curtains, so the sunlight can shine on him as it rises.

At 7:35 my mug is cold and empty but my grandmotherly anticipation still warm and overflowing.

I hear a familiar sound just outside the bedroom window. A Willie Wagtail has landed on the closest tree branch and starts whistling, calling to nearby friends.

Immediately two little eyes open, matched in beauty only by the subconscious smile of this city child, one so in tune with the native birdsong of rural Australia.

'It's time to feed the cows,' he utters as he drowsily climbs onto my lap to see his friend in the tree. And day two of our adventure begins.

Country love stars

There's one event that towns can't see.
Reserved for country; you and me.
It's not the moon in all its might
That shines its monthly cyclic light.
It's not the rare 'Cen-tury Red',
That moon is missed by those now dead.

    But fear it not, the news will cover
    Those that people won't discover.
    They see on screens and photos too
    The sights of telescopes with view.
    Of all things rare for probing looks
    Their information is from books.

The country folk know they stay there
The sky is filled with stars to share.
We see their grandeur every night
Once day has gone, and taken light.
With comfort knowing they'll return
The darkened hours yet to burn.

    The city lights – they hide the stars
    They may as well be far as Mars
    But man has built a wall between
    The heavens and the things unseen.
    Out in the bush, the view is clear
    As if to touch, they seem so near.

Simple things that keep us free
As humble as our life should be.
By nature, it helps us to rest,
Live our lives, and do our best.
It guides our cycles; helps earth grow,
All from glory's nightly show.

    But we aren't selfish; we will share
    We only wish you'd come and stare.
    So bring your swag, forget your torch
    And find a swing or country porch.
    Then just look up at stars above
    And know why country folk know love.

About the author:

Sandra Joy is a motivational writer who believes that our experiences, good and bad, are for the purpose of helping others.

Previous publications:

- Co-edited *Memory in Lockdown: Creative Nonfiction 2021*
- Published in *Memory in Lockdown: Creative Nonfiction 2021*
- Self-published *Salvation Through the Gift of Help 2020*
- Odyssey House Writing Competition 3rd place in 2019
- Published in *Beneath the Surface 2018*

Community involvement:

- Co-convenor of Alice Sinclair Memorial Writing Competition 2022
- Guest speaker at Lake Macquarie Write Here Festival 2022
- Guest speaker at Fellowship of Australian Writers Lake Macquarie branch April 2022
- Guest speaker at UON Children's Literature class 2021

Current studies:

- Bachelor of Arts, University of Newcastle, majoring in English & Writing, minoring in Writing Studies, and Education (3rd year)

Relevant networks and contacts:

- Fellowship of Australian Writers – member
- Newcastle Writers Festival – volunteer
- University of Newcastle – student
- Curtin University – student
- Hunter Writers Centre – placement student
- Write Here Festival – speaker
- Australian Publishers Association – micropublisher member

LIFE: a variant of adventure

Life does not always go to plan. It is not always easy or fun. It's just a process we go through – until we die. But that doesn't have to be morbid and scary, or funny and carefree.

What we experience in our life makes us who we are – the strong, resilient, powerful person who has earned the ability to have empathy to help others.

This collection of short stories spans over the phases of life one has endured. Topics include dating, addiction, violence, love, respect, heaven, alienation, death and more.

It is not an autobiography, just a sampler of life and some of the paths it can take.

These stories will make you laugh and cry – that's just life: a variant of adventure.

Appreciate the wonderful diverse you that your life has created.

www.ingramcontent.com/pod-product-compliance
Lightning Source LLC
Chambersburg PA
CBHW032150020426
42334CB00016B/1257